STEPNOTES™:

*The Counselor's Guide
to Progress Notes*

Rhonda Sutton
PH.D, LPC, LPC-S

Table of Contents

Foreword

Progress notes are crucial to every mental health practitioner's professional endeavors. Still, those who train counselors often fail to emphasize progress notes. I realized this as well as many other concerns about progress notes during my experiences as a licensed counselor and supervisor. This led me to create a clearer, more efficient way to take progress notes: a method I call STEPnotes™. I have written this book to help both counselors and counselors-in-training conceptualize their therapy sessions so that they can produce clear, thoughtful, and ethical progress notes for all of their clients.

Especially during my early experiences as a counselor, I wondered about my documentation on clients and their progress. I asked myself a lot of questions. I thought: Am I writing enough; am I writing too much; did I miss anything; what would an attorney think about my notes; how would the law construe my notes; how would an employee at an insurance company interpret my notes? I asked myself those, and many other questions, and found I was not alone in my curiosity and confusion. I realized that many counselors and counselors-in-training, especially those who are new to the profession, have these same concerns and questions.

As a supervisor to counselors-in-training, I frequently find that supervisees ask questions about taking good progress notes. My supervisees want me to review and make sure they are recording their progress notes correctly. The documentation mental health practitioners keep on their clients is critical to the practitioners' work. However, knowing the best way to maintain progress notes has been an elusive concept for many in counseling. For these reasons and others, I have given a lot of thought to developing STEPnotes™ as a clear, systematic way to document the therapy work that takes place between the counselor and client.

Reflecting on my education and experience, I created the concept for STEPnotes™. It is my sincere hope that other mental health providers—counselors, social workers, psychologists, marriage and family therapists, and all those who are in the therapy business—will find STEPnotes™ to be a helpful tool for producing progress notes.

Introduction

"A good set of progress notes is like a map for a counseling professional—a map that reveals roadblocks to progress and discloses the direction in which the therapy is going."

Most counselors and mental health professionals enjoy face-to-face interactions with their clients. Therapists work in this field so they can help people who are suffering emotionally. In order to alleviate their clients' suffering, counselors use varied therapeutic methods, devise treatment plans, and assess well-being.

These acts—listening, helping, processing, reframing, and guiding—can help counselors and clients work out issues. As a mental health professional, it is rewarding to apply new therapeutic tools, try different interventions, and watch clients improve. At the end of the day, counselors truly want to help their clients become better, but this process must occur both inside and outside the session.

Mental health providers who are thoughtful about their documentation have a better opportunity to help their clients. Progress notes help counselors offer aid to their clients. Taking the happenings of the session and putting them into words helps the therapist between sessions and over the course of the therapy with the client. A good set of progress notes is like a map for a counseling professional—a map that reveals roadblocks to progress and discloses the direction in which the therapy is going.

Should counseling professionals have a structured, consistent way to take progress notes? Yes, at least for the purpose of clarity, efficiency, and evaluation. The main goal of this book is to educate counselors and counselors-in-training about the ways they should conceptualize therapy sessions with clients, i.e. how they can produce effective, methodical progress notes. This book will provide readers with the STEPs™ to taking progress notes.

Conceptualizing therapy sessions makes it easier for counselors to thoughtfully evaluate each session in context. Counselors can plan and adjust future sessions according to their noted observations. With an organized manner of recording progress notes, counselors can easily identify reoccurring themes and clinical symptoms in their clients. Conceptualizing sessions involves more than just writing down what clients say. Noting both verbal responses and nonverbal behaviors is important as to assess the client's overall level of functioning. Documenting therapeutic interventions and theoretical orientations helps the counselor determine if the tactics being utilized are productive.

Given the labile moods and behaviors counselors often see in clients with mental health issues, counselors should evaluate their clients' current functioning and note improvements and declines in activity. Therapists should document how and when they have implemented treatment plans. Effective progress notes also assess progress towards counseling goals.

Counselors need to find the right words to document the therapy session in a truthful manner. They often do not know how much to write, and are concerned with what they should and should not include. There is always the possibility that an insurance company will audit a counselor on behalf of a client's insurance plan. It is also possible that an attorney will subpoena a mental health provider for official court proceedings. In those situations, counselors must have organized, well-formatted, and effectively documented notes.

Without a standardized way of producing progress notes, the process and its results are unpredictable. Counselors may produce illegible notes, fail to organize their progress notes, or may misplace progress notes. With all of these very real possibilities, progress notes can become the bane of a therapist's work. That is why counselors would benefit from using STEPnotes™. STEPnotes™ is systematic and efficient; it provides structure and gives counselors the ability to take control of their progress notes.

This book discusses each of the "STEPs™" in STEPnotes™ and provides a case study demonstrating how to conceptualize the various steps so that counselors can document the information from their therapy sessions. I will also include examples of the words and phrases one might use with each of the STEPs™.

Before we continue, we will first examine progress notes a little more. We will learn why they are a critical component of a mental health provider's work. The work completed during the counseling session is useful, but documenting this work (and having the ability to refer back to it) offers an otherwise unattainable advantage to counselors in assessing and providing care for their clients.

Chapter 1:
Why Progress Notes Are
Important to Counselors

"The main purpose of a progress note is to document the session in a way that reveals the client's needs and the type of therapy the counselor undertakes to meet those needs."

Mental health clinicians talk about writing progress notes, sometimes without knowing exactly what comprises progress notes. What are progress notes? Progress notes are the documented source of each counseling session; they are records of the therapeutic work that occurs between a counselor and a client. First, simply for record keeping, progress notes should include, but not be limited to, the following information:

- Name of the client
- Date of the session
- Length of the session (i.e., how many minutes the session lasted; CPT code)
- Type of session (e.g. individual counseling session, couples counseling session, family session, group session)
- Where the session occurred (in office, by phone, in home, in the community, other)
- Information about the client's presentation
- Information on the topics covered during the session
- What, if any, therapeutic actions were performed
- Diagnosis code for the client (obtained from either the DSM-5 or the ICD-10)
- The counselor's signature
- Date progress note was taken

Mental health providers can take many approaches to writing progress notes. Some clinicians jot down a few thoughts and file them in a folder. Others take notes on their computer. Some may write out as much of the session's dialogue as possible. There are even some in the mental health field that barely keep progress notes at all. A standardized progress note format ensures proficiency and ethics for all counselors. There are many other reasons why counselors should take reliable and thorough progress notes.

One of the main reasons to take high-quality progress notes is to allow the counselor to formulate a reason (or reasons) why a client needs counseling services. Reflecting upon the information gathered during a session can help clinicians determine diagnoses, treatment plans, goals, interventions, and courses of therapy. The verbal and non-verbal exchanges provide counselors with the details and insights they need to informatively and ethically assist clients. The main purpose of a progress note is to document the session in a way that reveals the client's needs and the type of therapy the counselor undertakes to meet those needs.

A second reason to take good progress notes is to understand the state of the therapy. Progress notes show the clinician how therapy is going for the client thus far. For example, good progress notes will inform clinicians whether clients are improving or regressing. By using effective progress notes, therapists can see if clients are focusing on the same topics each session. Clinicians can realize whether their clients exhibit similar symptoms each session or if their clients' levels of functioning are improving. Progress notes help clinicians answer questions like:

- Is the client open to or resistant to therapy?
- Is the client engaging in counseling or is there some level of guardedness in the client's presentation?
- Is the client making positive change, or is the client stuck?

The therapist needs to answer these questions as the therapy progresses. Otherwise, the client may continue to suffer or, worse, may even decompensate. The counselor must attend to subtle aspects of the sessions. Some things that may appear to be trivial are actually imperative to the therapy.

Progress notes are important for a third reason. They serve administrative functions for the therapist. Despite confidentiality and HIPPA regulations, insurance agencies and legal establishments may review a mental health provider's files. Insurance companies have the right to audit progress notes to figure out when therapy sessions are taking place and what occurs during the treatment process. Since insurance companies may pay a clinician for his or her work, they have the right to know if and how a client is receiving services. Also, if a client applies for disability, then the insurance company may review the counselor's progress notes to determine whether the client is eligible to receive disability benefits. If the legal system is involved then confidentiality may also be waived. Attorneys can subpoena therapists in order to obtain information for court cases. Having clear notes showing consistent record keeping and objective information reflects well on the counselor and indicates his or her professionalism.

An important point about progress notes: Progress notes are the notes mental health providers maintain that may, and likely will at some point, be open to insurance companies and/or subpoenaed. Some professionals may refer to these as the "clinical notes" in a client's file. For the purposes of this book I use the term "progress notes," which refers to the notes that may be audited, subpoenaed, or released to either the client or others involved in the client's care or situation.

"Psychotherapy notes" are different from progress notes; counselors should separate these from progress notes as these notes contain information that should not be shared or disclosed to third parties. Psychotherapy notes contain the therapist's written impressions and thoughts regarding the counseling session as well as the therapist's observations, clinical concerns and other anecdotal information about the client. Usually psychotherapy notes are private and are not subject to release, audit or subpoena. A mental health provider should be careful about storing these notes in any type of web-based or cloud-based system. Not all therapists keep separate notes on a session and may choose only to keep progress notes; this is entirely the decision of the individual practitioner.

All mental health providers need to be mindful to document the <u>objective</u> evaluation and <u>facts</u> within their progress notes. Counselors need to beware not to include their own subjective views or interpretations of the client or session, as progress notes may be subject to release.

An additional word about progress notes: mental health providers must maintain HIPAA compliance in regards to the security of their notes. This means keeping written progress notes and client files in a locked file cabinet. If notes are typed and stored on a computer or with an online electronic health records system, the clinician's computer needs to be encrypted as so to ensure security.

Clearly, progress notes are vital to the work of counselors and other mental health providers. Progress notes serve as a way to evaluate the course of therapy, determine what is and is not working with the client, and monitor the impact of counseling interventions as well as the client's overall functioning. Progress notes document when and for how long a counselor met with a client. These notes establish a record of the therapy. Whether the progress notes serve as records for the counselor to review prior to each session, justification for insurance payment, or documentation utilized in legal proceedings, these notes are essential for all counselors.

STEPnotes™ is a specific, step-by-step way for counselors to take progress notes. STEPnotes™ is the most dependable way to note a client's progress given its streamlined format and efficient layout. STEPnotes™ is available in both paper and e-tool formats. This system offers a great benefit for counselors and provides a professional way to record therapy sessions. The following chapters provide specific information on each of the STEPs™ and how to apply these STEPs™ when documenting a client's progress.

Chapter 2:
The STEPs™ to Taking Progress Notes

"To grasp each of the STEPs™ in context, you will assume the role of counselor to Miranda—the client of this fictional case study."

STEPnotes is the way to effectively conceptualize and document the work that occurs during counseling sessions. The STEPs™ in STEPnotes™ provide the underlying structure for progress notes along with a solid foundation for how to assess, evaluate, and plan treatments, interventions and goals for clients.

To help readers understand the STEPnotes™ method, I have provided the following fictional case study. To grasp each of the STEPs™ in context, you will assume the role of counselor to Miranda—the client of this fictional case study. I will refer to this case study and the STEPs™ described within it. Please note that all of the details provided in this case study are imagined and fictitious; any likeness to any real person or event is purely coincidental.

Case Study: Miranda

Following is information regarding Miranda, obtained from the intake session and other paperwork. This information provides the foundation for future progress notes and helps establish and monitor counseling goals for this fictional client. For the intent of this exercise you will act as counselor for Miranda.

Background of the Client

Miranda is a 42 year-old White woman. She ran a successful business as a consultant and motivational speaker before experiencing a major life transition. Miranda's professional background is in human resources and employee relations. Miranda is 5'7" tall, slender, blonde and blue-eyed. Miranda started seeing a counselor due to her recent health and relationship problems.

Miranda is married to Thomas, a 43 year-old medical surgeon who specializes in treating cancer patients. Thomas is African-American. He grew up poor. He was academically gifted and attained scholarships for college. He attended one of the most prestigious public universities in the South. There he received both his undergraduate and medical degrees.

Miranda and Thomas met in college during their junior years, and they have been together ever since. They have been married for twenty years and together (including time dating) for twenty-five years. They live in the same southern town where they got their college degrees, and they both have been very successful in their occupations. Miranda and Thomas have focused their lives on their careers and are quite wealthy, living in one of the most exclusive neighborhoods in their town.

Five months ago, Miranda went to the doctor due to some medical problems she was experiencing. The doctor found lumps in both of Miranda's breasts. Tests revealed an aggressive form of breast cancer. Due to the severity of the cancer, Miranda had a double mastectomy. Since that time, Miranda has closed down her consulting practice. She stays at home, and is focused on living a life she has never known— one of simplicity and solitude.

Miranda decided that she was living in an unhealthy way, so she took up gardening, and reading. She now enjoys a peaceful existence that includes meditation.

Miranda is seeking counseling because she is having problems with Thomas, both of a sexual nature and in regards to their overall communication. Before Miranda had a double mastectomy, Thomas and Miranda were very sociable and were "best friends." They would often go out with friends or have people over for dinner parties. Thomas is well respected among his peers at the hospital where he works, and he feels a certain need to socialize with the other doctors. Miranda is "not up for this" any more. Also, Miranda feels that Thomas no longer finds her attractive, and their intimacy has suffered.

Miranda wants to know what to do to make Thomas understand that she needs a "simple life." She wants to find a way to tell him what it has meant to her to have cancer. This seems especially difficult given that Thomas is a well-respected and successful oncologist. Thomas's cancer specialty is lymphoma. Miranda is still scared that the cancer will return, and she wants things in her life to change because she feels she has little time left.

Miranda, who has undergone aggressive radiation and chemotherapy, has been told that her prognosis is good and that her cancer is in remission, but Miranda still cannot shake the thoughts that her time now is very limited. Miranda thinks other people do not understand because she looks healthy (albeit rather thin). She did not lose her hair during treatment (but it did thin out), and she believes others think that since Thomas is an oncologist her recovery has gone well. Miranda regrets that she and Thomas never had children and, looking back on her life, the only thing she feels she has "accomplished" was making a lot of money and this, she claims, has not brought her any happiness.

During the intake session, Miranda appears calm and thoughtful. She relays the story of her experience having cancer and a double mastectomy in a soft, controlled manner. Miranda seems sad, but somewhat emotionally removed from the information she shares. Miranda says that she is focused on being at peace now. She still loves Thomas, but knows they are at "different places" given what she has recently gone through with her cancer treatment. Miranda sounds annoyed with her husband, at times, as she describes his need to continue life "the way it was" before she got cancer.

Second Session

When Miranda comes in for her second counseling session, she is wearing a well-tailored dress and high-heeled shoes. Her hair is neat and her fingernails are polished. However, Miranda appears sad and she shares that after the last session she had with you, she realized how lonely she feels. Thomas continues to play golf, and he is very frustrated that she will not go out to dinner with him and their friends. Thomas said that he must "keep making excuses" for her when it seems to him that she should be more engaged with people. Miranda starts to cry quietly, looking down and away from you, the counselor. She shakes her head, sharing that if Thomas does not understand what she is going through, what does this mean for the future of their marriage?

Miranda and Thomas have both always been independent, self-reliant and "fun". Miranda emphasizes this last word in a slightly sarcastic tone. She then looks up at you and states, "Being a victim of cancer isn't 'fun'—can't he see that? He works with people like me all day—can't he see me? Can't he see I am not what he married? I have cancer. I have been cut, and I am damaged. I have faced death. What is wrong with me that he can't see me—that he can't accept what I am now?" Miranda then begins to cry more. As the counselor, you allow her some time to cry. Then, when appropriate, you reflect that it seems Miranda still feels victimized by her cancer and that it must be hard not to be "seen" clearly by someone who not only loves her, but has specialized knowledge in the area that has caused her victimization. Miranda nods her head, "yes," and then proceeds to share, in a slightly annoyed and sarcastic way, that things are never truly how they may appear.

Miranda states she had this happy, idyllic life with Thomas, but now she is "damaged goods". All that she thought was good and true has come to an end, and what she thought she had—an understanding, compassionate, loving husband and a fulfilling life—is gone. Instead, Miranda believes Thomas is ashamed of her since he will not talk with her about the mastectomy. Miranda also feels reluctant to have Thomas touch her or be near her because she herself can hardly stand to look at herself in front of the mirror, even from the neck up. Miranda states that she sees how cancer has "ravaged" her— wrinkles in her face, thinned hair, no breasts, and a drastic loss of weight and muscle tone.

Miranda used to run, and play tennis. She used to feel good about her body and liked showing it off. She wore low-back dresses to social functions and bikinis on the trips she and Thomas took to the Caribbean. Miranda also sees how the support she thought she had in friends is not there. She continues that "it seems as if they think cancer is contagious...no one calls me or asks me how I'm doing...I am just supposed to go back to being who I was...so I just stay away from them. No one wants to be near me, and no one understands." Miranda shakes her head sadly and sighs, with her eyes cast down and her fingers nervously twisting the tissue in her hand.

Following is the general format for STEPnotes™ as well as the ways in which to apply each of the STEPs™ to the counseling session. For the purposes of the STEPnotes™ example, picture yourself as the counselor working with Miranda, and, given the details of the intake and the second counseling sessions that have been offered here, you are encouraged to reflect upon how to use and conceptualize the information I discuss for each of the STEPs™. I will examine each of the STEPs™ using the sessions with Miranda as the model for the progress notes.

Chapter 3:
The First "STEP": S = Subject(s) and Symptoms

"Symptoms are key indicators of the type of diagnosis a counselor must give to the client; identifying symptoms helps the counselor decide how to treat the client."

The first "step" in STEPnotes™, "S," serves a two-fold purpose. The "S" indicates both the SUBJECTS the client discusses as well as the SYMPTOMS the client reports or exhibits.

Subjects are the areas of discussion from the session. They are the issues on which the client focuses during the session. The subject also consists of what the client has been experiencing outside of the session. The client may discuss one subject, or may bring up many. The counselor should recognize whether the subjects are the same session-to-session or if subjects fluctuate between the sessions. One subject may trigger memories of other experiences, so it is not unusual for a client to seek counseling for one reason and then later start to explore other issues and subjects. Examples of possible subjects include, but are not limited to:

- Addiction
- Anxiety
- Behavioral problems
- Body image issues
- Depression
- Divorce
- Eating disorder
- Health problems
- Grief

- Legal problems
- Life transition(s)
- Marital discord
- Parenting issues
- Physical abuse
- Regret
- Relationship problems
- School problems
- Self-esteem issues
- Self-harm
- Sexual intimacy issues
- Trauma

If the client reveals other issues, pay attention to those. Counselors should figure out whether new subjects arise from session-to-session. They should realize whether certain subjects prompt others. If new subjects arise, the therapist needs to take those into consideration with regard to counseling goals and treatment plans.

As the therapist, what would you choose as the subjects(s) Miranda focused on during her second session? Miranda clearly speaks on the subjects of grief, marital discord, and sexual intimacy issues. What underlying concerns may additionally exist? What can you, the counselor, infer from the statements Miranda makes? It sounds like she has self-esteem issues given the statements about her being "damaged goods". She also indicates a lack of a support system given her comments about her husband, Thomas, and her friends "not understanding" what she has been experiencing as a result of having breast cancer. Miranda also alludes to a sense of regret in her comments about how she used to be able to be active and go out with friends and now she cannot. During the intake session, Miranda also has some comments about not having children; these statements indicate a sense of regret as well. They may also indicate that Miranda is confused about her sense of purpose.

The second part of the "S" in STEPs™ refers to the symptoms. Clinicians need to be aware that symptoms include emotional, behavioral, cognitive and physical symptoms. This awareness allows clinicians to take a holistic perspective by noticing the clients' verbal and non-verbal expressions. The clinician may observe symptoms during the therapy session, or the client may self-report symptoms. In many cases both manners of attaining information about clients' symptoms occur. Just as the verbal exchange is important during the session, the clinician must note non-verbal aspects of the client's presentation as these can indicate deeper symptoms, worries, thoughts, or pains.

Emotional symptoms refer to the client's feelings during the course of the experience she or he is describing. Emotional symptoms may also refer to the emotional actions the client displays during the session. Emotional symptoms vary depending on the subject the client discusses during the session. If the counseling session includes more than one client, such as a couples or family session, it is important to observe the types of emotions that each client exhibits individually and towards other clients in the session. If the client is talking about someone who is not present (and that person may well be the impetus for the client seeking counseling), be sure to note the client's emotional responses to what she or he is sharing about that person. Examples of emotional symptoms include:

- Anger
- Annoyance
- Apathy
- Bereavement
- Bitter
- Confidence
- Confusion
- Despondence
- Devastation
- Disappointment
- Elation
- Exhaustion
- Frustration

- Relief
- Sadness
- Shame
- Tenseness

Given the information shared in the second session with Miranda, what are some of the emotional symptoms you would note about Miranda? From the details provided, it is evident that Miranda is annoyed and possibly even angry with her husband given her outburst during the session. Miranda shares that she is lonely due to what she perceives to be a lack of support from her friends and Thomas. Miranda expresses that she is sad about the changes to her body. It seems plausible that Miranda is angry that she had cancer and that it has taken so much away from her. Miranda is frustrated because she thinks no one understands how she feels and no one cares to find out.

Many of these emotions point to the potential diagnosis of depression for Miranda; it is also important to realize Miranda is experiencing grief, which is a normal response to loss. Given the intake information and second session details, are there other emotional symptoms you would attribute to Miranda?

Behavioral symptoms are non-verbal expressions the client displays during the course of the therapy. Behavior is often the expression of what one is experiencing on an emotional level. For example, an angry client may express their anger by speaking in a loud, agitated voice. Behavioral symptoms provide insight into the client's level of functioning, and one of the goals of therapy is to improve these behavioral symptoms so that the client's functioning improves. Keep in mind that behavioral symptoms not only impact the client, but these behaviors may also have a role in how the client is interacting with others. This, in turn, can lead to further problems for the client. Some examples of behavioral symptoms are:

- Agitation
- Alcohol use
- Crying
- Drug use
- Eating less
- Fleeting eye contact
- Hyper-vigilance
- Irrational behavior
- Loud speech
- Minimal eye contact
- Poor impulse control
- Shyness (of an atypical variety)
- Squandering

While some behaviors are normal for clients, clinicians should watch out for abnormal behaviors. For example, if a client typically speaks in a loud voice, then that may just be his or her usual inflection. Thus it likely does not imply anger as it may in other clients.

During the second session with Miranda, one of the behavioral symptoms she exhibits is crying. Crying indicates grief and sorrow. Miranda's cancer, the changes in her relationship with her husband, and the distance she feels from her friends and loved ones may contribute to Miranda's grief and sorrow. As the counselor, you may want to explore the reasons for her tears by allowing her the time to process the feelings she associates with weeping.

Several times during the session Miranda exhibits minimal or poor eye contact. This may indicate shame, embarrassment, or an overwhelming feeling in response to her many emotions. Ensuring that Miranda feels safe in the session is important. The counselor should note when Miranda begins to make more eye contact. This would likely indicate that Miranda is building confidence, comfort, and positive feelings about counseling and her relationship with you, the counselor.

Another behavior Miranda exhibits is isolation. She isolates herself from loved ones. This behavior probably affects her feelings of loneliness and sadness. The combination of these behaviors may indicate that Miranda is suffering from grief and possibly depression. Are there other behavioral symptoms you, as the counselor, can note from the intake information or second counseling session details?

A client's thoughts or cognitions reflect in the client's cognitive symptoms. Cognitive symptoms are defined by the following: the types of thoughts the client has, how the client processes information, and the way the client thinks about emotions, behaviors, and events. The cognitions a client reveals can indicate how well he or she is functioning. Serious cognitions that need immediate attention, like hallucinations and delusions, may be signs of psychosis. If a client consistently expresses anxious thoughts, these thoughts may imply past trauma or certain behavioral patterns. Cognitive symptoms include:

- Anxious thoughts
- Confusion
- Delusions
- Difficulty making decisions
- Hallucinations
- Irrational thoughts
- Memory problems
- Negative thoughts
- Poor judgment

- Racing thoughts
- Tangential thoughts

During Miranda's second session she shares many negative thoughts about her self-image, her marriage, and her friendships. Miranda may be confused about her life transitions and her current standpoint. She once had a fulfilling social life and career, but now stays at home meditating, gardening, and isolating herself from others. Miranda may also be experiencing some anxious thoughts about how others perceive her. In addition to these anxious thoughts, Miranda appears to have reservations about the state of her health. As she says, she is "still scared that the cancer will return." Uncertainty—about the state of her health and the future of her marriage—may contribute to Miranda's anxiety and potential depression. Given the details she shares from the intake and the second counseling sessions, does Miranda have any other cognitive symptoms?

Physical symptoms refer to the client's physical appearance as well as any health conditions the client reports. Given that there is a strong connection between the mind and the body, physical symptoms can provide the counselor with additional insights into the client's level of disturbance. Noting the client's physical presentation may be a key indicator of how the client is functioning. It is also useful to see, for example, if the well-groomed client is "masking" the true internal turmoil and emotional chaos she or he is experiencing. Knowing more about the client's physical problems can help the counselor devise treatment plans and therapy goals. As negative physical symptoms decrease, the client's level of functioning and overall well-being will likely improve and increase.

Physical symptoms and either reported or observed during the session may include:

- Back pain
- Constipation
- Disheveled appearance
- Hot flashes
- Indigestion
- Nausea
- Neat appearance
- Neck tension
- Rash
- Shortness of breath
- Skin irritations
- Ulcers
- Unclean appearance
- Unkempt appearance
- Well-groomed appearance

It seems no significant physical symptoms are disclosed or discussed in the second session with Miranda. She appears well groomed and mindful of her appearance. However, because Miranda is a cancer survivor who is expressing significant signs of grief and depression, it would be important for you, the counselor, to inquire about her sleep, her appetite and her level of energy. As the counselor, you may also want to explore more about what Miranda had to undergo for her cancer treatment and see if she is experiencing any effects from the radiation or chemotherapy. Even if a client does not disclose any physical symptoms, keep in mind that asking about these can provide a more holistic image of the client's current level of functioning.

A counselor needs to monitor all of the symptoms—emotional, behavioral, cognitive and physical—to see how these manifest over the course of the therapy. Symptoms are key indicators of the type of diagnosis a counselor must give to the client; identifying symptoms helps the counselor decide how to treat the client. A decrease in the negative symptoms indicates that the client is improving. An increase in the positive symptoms shows that counseling is helping.

Chapter 4:
The Second Step: "T" = Therapeutic Tools

"Noting in the progress notes the tools and actions that the therapist implemented during the session can help the therapist evaluate which therapeutic modalities work best."

"T" refers to the THERAPEUTIC TOOLS the counselor utilizes during the session with the client. This section of the progress note is especially important for insurance companies, for this part specifies the therapy and interventions the counselor implements with the client. Insurance companies can and do audit mental health providers. Insurance agents will likely scrutinize this section. The first part of therapeutic tools refers to the therapy approach or approaches the counselor uses. Examples of therapy approaches are:

- Cognitive-behavioral therapy
- Narrative therapy
- Person-centered therapy
- Reality therapy
- Solution-focused therapy

Some counselors use conventional approaches whereas others are more eclectic in their therapy work. It is important that counselors understand the therapeutic approaches and how these approaches guide their counseling and client interventions.

A client may benefit if the counselor uses various therapeutic approaches as opposed to a singular approach. A counselor may note more than one therapeutic approach in a progress note for a particular session. A counselor may also note different therapeutic approaches in different sessions. The same counseling approach is not necessarily used with the same client during every session. However, if a counselor has been using a certain approach, such as person-centered, for a number of sessions and then decides to implement another approach, such as cognitive-behavioral techniques, the counselor should inform the client of the change. Obviously the counselor should also note this shift in the progress notes. A counselor who uses many and varied therapeutic approaches may want to share this fact with the client during the intake session.

The ability to identify and note the therapeutic approach in the progress note is essential; also essential to the progress note are the actions the therapist takes during the session with the client. The reason for this is that the actions the counselor implements during the session reveal whether the therapy is working for the client. Noting statements, interventions, and exchanges between the practitioner and the client also demonstrates the professional aspects of their work. For this part of the therapeutic tools section, counselors need to use action verbs in order to document the work they carry out with their clients. This makes it clear that both the therapist and the client are engaged in an active therapeutic relationship. Action verbs such as the following are helpful in illustrating this relationship:

- Acknowledged
- Addressed
- Aligned
- Demonstrated
- Encouraged
- Explored
- Illustrated
- Normalized
- Observed
- Processed
- Reframed
- Reflected
- Verbalized

These are all examples of action verbs that can help describe how the therapist puts the theoretical approach or approaches into practice. These words reveal what the counselor did and how these actions impacted the client or influenced the course of therapy. These actions also show that the counselor did much more than just listen to the client. Anyone can listen; therapists are skilled professionals who use various methods and tools to guide clients through processes of stabilizing, improving, and healing. Counseling is supposed to help a client through a difficult time, but the client cannot do this alone.

The counselor needs to indicate what he or she did to facilitate processing, learning, and application of insights and tools.

Assume the role of Miranda's counselor during the second session. Given the information as to how Miranda presents herself and what she shares in the second session, what counseling approach or approaches would you take with her?

Since this is the second session, would you want to utilize the person-centered approach to continue building rapport and establishing a sense of trust in the therapeutic relationship? Would you find it more beneficial to apply narrative therapy techniques so as to better understand how Miranda's former life and her experience with cancer have shaped her? Do you think it would be best to employ cognitive-behavioral strategies by focusing on how Miranda's thoughts impact her feelings?

Upon reflecting on the second counseling session with Miranda, the counselor may write out sentences similar to the following in order to take note of actions taken during the session:

- I acknowledged Miranda's feelings of loneliness, anger and shame.
- I defined how things "truly appear" for Miranda

- I explored Miranda's verbalizations about being a "victim" of cancer.
- Miranda indicated that she feels out of control regarding the changes to her body.
- I normalized Miranda's feelings of anger and frustration, and the impact these had on her.
- I processed Miranda's feelings about herself and her husband to better understand how the marriage has recently changed.
- I reframed for Miranda the fact that she has survived cancer.
- I worked to identify her cancer survival (as well as other events) as strengths.

Noting in the progress notes the tools and actions that the therapist implements during the session can help the therapist evaluate which therapeutic methods work best. Some clients may respond better to more directive theoretical approaches, whereas others need time to process their thoughts and feelings. The sentences that describe responses, interventions and other work facilitate a clearer understanding of what is working with the client. These action verbs also indicate to outside sources—such as courts of law or insurance companies—the professional work occurring between the therapist and client.

Chapter 5:
The Third Step: "E" = Evaluation

"A counselor must be cautious when evaluating a client early in the counseling relationship. Gathering additional information allows the counselor to formulate a more accurate and appropriate diagnosis."

"E" is the EVALUATION section of the progress note. Evaluation involves the client's level of engagement in therapy; for example, whether the client is:

- Engaged in therapy
- Guarded
- Minimizing
- Open
- Stuck

The goal with this part of the evaluation is to ascertain if the client is working towards their counseling goals or if something is occurring that inhibits the counseling process. Also, does the client's response to therapy change with each session or is the client relatively engaged in the same manner each session? This part of the STEPs™ reveals the type of relationship and trust established between the therapist and the client. The therapeutic relationship is a central component to successful counseling. If a client becomes unengaged or guarded after having exhibited trust towards the counselor it is vital to note when this occurred and discovering, if possible, what caused the change in the relationship. Once trust is established, the counselor can work effectively.

Other issues regarding the evaluation of a client's engagement in therapy are related to the client's level of functioning. For example, a client may have difficulty engaging due to psychosis, any medical condition that exacerbates cognitive problems, or a lack of mental capacity. This section of the STEPs™ helps the counselor identify critical aspects of the counseling session, which in turn allows the counselor to establish future counseling needs and approaches.

EVALUTION also needs to include an assessment of the client's current level of functioning. Find a guide to this assessment at the back of this book. You will evaluate the client's functioning using the information shared and the interactions experienced. The scale runs from 1 to 10, with 1 being very poor functioning and 10 being optimal functioning. For example, a client who comes to therapy and appears disheveled, has difficulty expressing thoughts, and has not been to work in the last three days due to delusions is more than likely at a "1" or a "2" on this scale. A client who has learned coping skills for anxiety, who has implemented these successfully for the past six weeks, and who is now able to attend social functions and engage in healthy relationships with members of his or her support system is probably at an "8," "9," or "10". Find in the back of this book the STEPnotes™ scale to use when determining a client's current level of functioning.

One purpose of this evaluation is to assess whether or not the client is in the proper care of mental health treatment. A client who is at the lower end of the scale may need more intensive or even in-patient treatment. A client who has moved up the scale during the course of therapy to a "9" or a "10" is more than likely at a point where therapy can be reduced or, if appropriate, concluded. Recognizing the level of care a client needs is important in the overall evaluation, and this scale provides not only a quantitative designation of the client's current level of functioning but also an assessment of the client's current level of therapeutic needs.

This assessment is of particular importance when working with clients who share suicidal or homicidal ideation, as well as with those clients with serious concerns involving depression, anxiety, hallucinations, delusions and poor self-care. If the client has expressed suicidal ideation (SI) or homicidal ideation (HI), it is imperative that the counselor indicate if a contract for safety was made, if the client was admitted to a hospital, or if law enforcement was involved as detailed records need to be maintained when SI or HI are reported Also, if there is reason to suspect child or elder abuse, the counselor must address and note when he or she contacts the proper authorities.

The last part of the evaluation section refers to the DSM diagnoses. It is important to note the DSM diagnoses for these may change over the course of counseling as counselors gain new information about their clients. If a diagnosis does change, then the counselor may need to modify the treatment plan and counseling goals.

Recalling the intake and second sessions with Miranda, examine the first part of the evaluation step and assess Miranda's level of engagement in the therapeutic process as well as her level of functioning. Keep in mind that this is only the second session with Miranda, thus you will want to consider the level of rapport you have built with her. Clients often experience an increase in their levels of engagement and openness as their counseling relationships develop. Counselors may need to think about what it means if a client is very open during the first couple of sessions or if the client is extremely guarded; these behaviors tend to provide insight into the client's personality and level of functioning. From the intake session, it appears that Miranda is somewhat guarded given her "calm" manner when responding to questions. Also she does not show much emotion regarding her recent experience with breast cancer. However, given the information about Miranda during the second session, it seems she is feeling fairly comfortable with you, the counselor. She goes from quietly crying to looking at you while sharing some rather painful thoughts and feelings. Therefore, Miranda is "open" at this time, at least in terms of her willingness to share during the counseling session. As the counselor, is there anything else you would add in terms of her level of engagement in therapy? One may need more information to determine if she is stuck or guarded about certain aspects of her experiences.

Now we will examine the next part of the evaluation for Miranda using the STEPnotes™ Client's Current Level of Functioning Scale. Find this scale at the back of the book. Information from the intake and the second counseling session with Miranda indicates that she is exhibiting symptoms of grief and or depression. It also appears that she is having a difficult time in her marriage and social relationships. In addition, Miranda drastically closed her consulting business and is no longer engaged in any type of employment. Miranda has radically changed the structure of her life to one of seclusion by reading books, staying at home, and gardening. The couple has no financial concerns, so the fact that Miranda is unemployed is not a financial issue. However, the counselor should note as serious that Miranda's life has shifted from a life engaged with others to a life of isolation. This life transition provides information about Miranda's current level of functioning. You, as the counselor, may want to place her level of functioning between a "5" and a "6" on the scale provided. Also, it is important to document in your progress notes that Miranda is not disclosing any suicidal ideation or homicidal ideation. Be sure to apply the information gathered from this evaluation and that from your own observations to formulate the client's diagnosis when reviewing the DSM-5.

The final part of the evaluation portion of the progress note involves the diagnosis. Information and observations from the intake and the second counseling sessions indicate that Miranda:

- May be experiencing a depressed mood during most of the day due to her isolation from others and her lack of communication and intimacy with her husband.
- Has a markedly diminished interest in activities that she used to enjoy such as traveling with Thomas and/or spending time with their friends.
- Feelings of worthlessness given her comments about how she looks and how breast cancer has "damaged" her.
- Possible psychomotor retardation given that she has "slowed down" and is not engaging in life the way she did prior to her cancer treatment.
- Thoughts of death or dying given her concerns about the cancer returning.

These, symptoms, as referred to in the DSM-5, indicate a possible diagnosis of Adjustment Disorder with Depressed Mood (309.0). However, the counselor may want to rule out Major Depressive Disorder, Mild, Single Episode (296.21) by gathering additional information about her mood during the day, her engagement in activities, her thoughts about death, and her feelings about lifestyle changes. A counselor must be cautious when evaluating a client early in the counseling relationship. Gathering additional information allows the counselor to formulate a more accurate and appropriate diagnosis.

With regards to Miranda, it is important to note that gardening, reading books and meditating are activities that she may find pleasurable. These activities may be more in line with how she wants to live her life now that she has experienced breast cancer. However, the counselor should find out more about the extent of these activities as well as about how Miranda feels about the major changes in her life.

Chapter 6:
The Fourth Step: "P" = Plan

"The plan section of STEPnotes™ establishes continuity and context regarding treatment, goals, and interventions and their effectiveness."

"P" stands for PLAN. It is the last of the STEPs™ in STEPnotes™. It refers to the short and long-term plans developed during the course of the therapy, the overall goal of which is to improve the client's well-being. Plans can include homework, interventions, and long-term goals. Plans can also include topics or other details that were not discussed during a session, things that may call for a follow-up. Topics may arise during a session but may not be fully addressed due to time constraints or the need to focus on other issues. Counselors should develop plans that ensure clients are striving towards and meeting short and long-term goals in a focused manner. Plans will vary from counselor to counselor, depending on the counseling approach. For example, a cognitive-behavioral therapist may use different types of homework assignments than those of the practitioner who employs narrative counseling techniques.

It is essential for a sense of rapport to have focused goals that are established by both the client and the therapist. Therapists should write down these goals in the plan portion of the notes in a way that will hopefully integrate the clients' goals with the therapeutic work. Examples of how these types of statements may begin include, but are not limited to the following:

- Client will acknowledge...
- Client will address...

- Client will attend…
- Client will build…
- Client will change…
- Client will communicate…
- Client will decrease…
- Client will develop…
- Client will draw…
- Client will exhibit…
- Client will explore…
- Client will express…
- Client will gain…
- Client will identify…
- Client will implement…
- Client will improve…
- Client will increase…
- Client will list…
- Client will maintain…
- Client will manage…
- Client will monitor…
- Client will practice…
- Client will process…
- Client will reduce…
- Client will replace…
- Client will share…
- Client will show…

- Client will structure…
- Client will utilize…
- Client will verbalize…
- Client will write…

The counselor can replace "client" with the client's name or restructure the above phrases to suit particular needs. The important part of these statements is that they involve future and goal-oriented verbs.

As Miranda's counselor, what types of information would you include in the plan section of your STEPnotes™ progress notes? Following are some suggestions for a counselor who uses cognitive-behavioral and person-centered approaches to counseling:

- Miranda feels victimized, damaged and "ravaged"; she is clearly experiencing a lot of grief and anger. One homework assignment for Miranda: **she will write** a letter to her cancer describing her feelings about the cancer and what it has taken from her. With this assignment, hopefully **Miranda will process** her thoughts as feelings. The intent of this assignment is to help her move through her grief.
- As a statement in the plan section: **Client will write** a letter to her cancer with the goal of exploring her feelings. Hopefully the **client will process** her feelings

and thoughts with regard to what she has endured as a result of her cancer.

- Miranda states that she is lonely. Given Miranda's level of isolation from friends, a goal should be to increase her engagement with others. **Client will get involved** with others, either with those who are her friends, or with those who share her new interests of gardening, meditation or reading. It may also be helpful for Miranda to join a support group for those who have survived breast cancer so that she can decrease her feelings of not being understood and connect to those who have gone through a similar experience.

- As a statement in the plan section: **Client will increase** her social support system by becoming involved in support group for breast cancer survivors or by joining groups that involve her personal interests.

- Miranda's marriage appears to be in a critical state. Help Miranda identify what she would like to say to her husband, Thomas. Work with her to determine ways to assertively share her thoughts, feelings, and needs.

- As a statement in the plan section: **Client will share** her thoughts, feelings, and needs with her husband using assertive techniques.

- Miranda has made some significant changes in her life. Overall she seems to possess some strong resiliency skills, given her former work and her current decisions about what she needs. Another goal is to work with Miranda to identify her strengths, to change her negative thoughts into more positive ones about what she has endured and survived, and to help her to continue to utilize positive coping strategies as she moves through her grief and acceptance of the changes she has experienced.

- As a statement in the plan section: **Client will identify** her strengths so as to help her cope with what she has endured as a result of the cancer. **Client will develop** positive cognitions to replace negative thoughts so that she can move towards accepting the changes she has experienced as a result of the cancer.

- For the next session, be sure to check in with Miranda about her homework assignment, the letter to the cancer. Provide a list of local resources that focus on supporting those who have survived breast cancer. Determine three changes Miranda wants to see in her life as a result of counseling.

The plan section of the progress notes assists the therapist in two ways. First, the plan statements establish goals for counseling and monitor effectiveness of the interventions in meeting these goals. Secondly, the information in the plan part of STEPnotes™ provides a guide from session to session. The mental health practitioner should review the plan section before every meeting.

The plan section of STEPnotes™ establishes continuity and context regarding treatment, goals, and interventions and their effectiveness. Clients do not necessarily recall what they discussed in prior sessions, and they may not be able to realize their own progress (or lack of progress). Therefore, it is incumbent upon the mental health provider to note progress. The counseling professional must use his or her skills to monitor the client's progress, to evaluate the efficacy of the counseling process, and to determine the necessary therapeutic tools to assist and support the client in reaching her or his goals. The plan portion of the progress note assists the therapist with this type of evaluation and this section plays a significant role in providing continuity needed for effective treatment throughout the therapy process.

Following is how the finalized version of the STEPnotes™ for the second session with Miranda would appear:

STEPnotes™ Individual Counseling Progress Note

Client Name:
Miranda Z.

Session Date:
Thursday, August 15 2013

Session Length:
45 minutes

CPT Code:
90834 (counseling session – actual time of 38 to 52 minutes)

STEP 1: S = Subjects and Symptoms
Subject(s) Discussed:

- Anger
- Communication problems
- Grief/loss
- Health problems
- Marital discord
- Problems with friends
- Self-esteem issues
- Sexual problems

More Details of Subject(s) Discussed:

Client has survived breast cancer and double mastectomy. She is currently dealing with grief over the bodily changes she has experienced as a result of the cancer. She is having both communication problems and intimacy issues with her husband. Feels her friends do not understand and appears to lack a support system to deal with the aftermath of cancer treatment and surgery. Has made significant changes in her life; abandoned her career and is now "living a life of solitude." Client seems to be experiencing some regrets over not having children and putting so much time, energy and effort into the career she had before she was diagnosed with cancer.

Emotional Symptoms:

- Angry
- Annoyed
- Confused
- Depressed
- Fearful
- Frustrated
- Hurt
- Lonely
- Negative
- Rejected
- Sad
- Scared

- Upset

Behavioral Symptom(s):

- Crying
- Isolating from others
- Minimal eye contact

Cognitive Symptom(s):

- Anxious thoughts
- Confusion
- Negative thoughts

Physical Symptom(s):

- Well-groomed appearance

STEP 2: T = Therapeutic Tools
Therapy Approach(es) Used:

- Cognitive-Behavioral Therapy (CBT)
- Narrative Therapy
- Person-Centered Therapy

Tools Utilized:

- Acknowledged Miranda's feelings of loneliness, anger and shame
- Defined how things "truly appear" now for Miranda
- Explored Miranda's verbalizations about being a "victim" of cancer
- Identified Miranda's survival as a strength that Miranda has exhibited with her cancer treatments
- Normalized Miranda's feelings of anger and frustration as well as the impact these have had on her
- Processed Miranda's feelings about herself and her husband so as to obtain a better understanding of the current state of the marriage
- Reframed for Miranda all she has done to survive cancer – negative thoughts to positive cognitions

STEP 3: E = EVALUATION

Evaluation:
Client is open; willing to share emotions/thoughts.

Assessment of Functioning Scale:
"5": Moderate Level of Functioning; Goals are Being Set

DSM Diagnosis:
309.0: Adjustment disorder with depressed mood

STEP 4: P = PLAN

Plan:

- Client will write a letter to her cancer describing her feelings towards it, what it has taken from her.
- Client will be encouraged to process her feelings so as to help her move through the grief process.
- Client will get involved with others to build social support system.
- Client will share her thoughts, feelings and needs with her husband using assertive techniques.
- Client will identify her strengths so as build and strengthen her coping skills.
- Client will develop positive cognitions to replace negative thoughts.

Additional information about plan:

For the next session, check in with Miranda about her homework assignment, the letter to the cancer. Provide her with a list of local resources that focus on supporting those who have survived breast cancer. Determine three (3) changes Miranda wants to see in her life as a result of counseling.

Chapter 7:
STEPnotes™ for the 21st Century: The Electronic Format

"The online version of STEPnotes™ serves to provide mental health professionals with the most effective smart tools for assessing, evaluating, and planning actions, interventions and goals for clients."

Following the outline of the STEPs™ helps counselors conceptualize their therapy and document the work that takes place during sessions. As is, STEPnotes™ streamlines how counselors take progress notes. Additionally, STEPnotes™, Inc. has created an e-tool that can save practitioners time and effort. The goal of STEPnotes™ is to provide counselors and other mental health professionals a smart tool to take progress notes.

With the online version of STEPnotes™, users have access to an intake form, and can scan and add additional documents (up to five separate entries) to each client's session. These documents might include release of information, journal entries, telephone messages, etc. The e-version of STEPnotes™ also helps counselors with their efficiency; counselors can easily retrieve their notes through the online, secure, HIPAA-compliant system from any desktop, laptop, tablet or mobile device. This e-tool eliminates the inconveniences of bulging files and illegible handwriting. The streamlined format makes it simple to keep notes in a manner that would be deemed therapeutic and professional by insurance companies and legal entities.

Following are the more specific "e-tool bonuses" for each of the STEPs™ found in the e-version of STEPnotes™.

Both the SUBJECTS and the SYMPTOMS in the STEPnotes™ online format consist of drop down menus. There are over 100 SUBJECTS from which to choose, plus users can also enter their own subjects. In the drop down menu for the SYMPTOMS categories, there are over 140 emotional symptoms, over 20 behavioral symptoms, over 15 cognitive symptoms, and over 30 physical symptoms. Users can always add more details and information regarding the SUBJECTS and SYMPTOMS; that way, drop down choices do not restrict users. When the counselor reviews the progress note for a particular session, the counselor will only see his or her typed information plus the options she or he has chosen to see.

The THERAPEUTIC TOOLS part of the online version of STEPnotes™ contains a menu of over twenty (20) therapy modalities, and the user can check as many as she or he wishes to indicate the various therapeutic approaches utilized in any particular session. There is also space to indicate any other therapy approaches that the counselor uses. In addition, there are over 70 action words from which to choose. The user simply completes a sentence using the chosen action verb(s) and can choose as many as he or she likes. When the counselor reviews the progress note for a particular session, only the therapy approaches selected and/or the action verb(s) along with the information filled in next to the words chosen will appear on the view/print form.

The EVALUATION section of the online version of STEPnotes™ contains a checklist of twelve (12) choices regarding the client's level of engagement in the counseling process; the user can check as many as she or he deems appropriate. The counselor can add additional information regarding the evaluation of the client's progress and can add additional information about how well (or how poorly) therapy is progressing for the client. For the assessment of functioning, the STEPnotes™ one-to-ten point slider scale is available for the user. A version of this scale is available at the end of this book.

The online version of STEPnotes™ allows for additional information about suicidal ideation (SI) or homicidal ideation (HI) in the EVALUATION section as well as a place to indicate the DSM diagnosis or diagnoses. The DSM diagnosis section will re-populate with each new STEPnotes™ completed on any client. That way, the user does not have to look up or recall the diagnosis code each time for a particular client. As is the case with the other sections of the e-version of STEPnotes™, only the information checked, chosen or typed will appear in the view/print format of the progress note.

The PLAN for each client should be very specific in nature. The PLAN section includes a menu to choose and indicate goals. Because each client is unique, the PLAN section of the online version of STEPnotes™ contains a box where the counselor can write in as much as he or she wants regarding the treatment plan and goals for future sessions. Counselors can also write in any other information pertinent to the plan for the client. It is helpful for the mental health provider to review the notes, particularly the plan section, prior to each session in order to maintain continuity, care, and focus.

To find out more about STEPnotes™ and how this HIPAA-compliant, online format may benefit mental health providers, visit stepnotesinc.com. The online version of STEPnotes™ serves to provide mental health professionals with the most effective smart tools for assessing, evaluating, and planning actions, interventions and goals for clients. Plans for individual therapists start at $15 per month. Feedback is always welcome. Contact the STEPnotes™ team at info@stepnotesinc.com for more information.

Chapter 8:
STEPnotes™ for School and Career Counselors

"The school and career counseling options of STEPnotes™ offer the same streamlined features of the original online version, but in addition consider domain-specific issues."

STEPnotes™ not only offers online progress notes for individual mental health counselors, but also customized online progress note options for career counselors and school counselors.

School Counseling STEPnotes™ offers choices associated with the American School Counselor Association (ASCA) standards. These options are available under the TOOLS section of the note. Noting these standards will help schools that want to achieve the RAMP designation. That is because school counselors will have available the data regarding the work they do and the ASCA National Standards. Subjects specific to school settings appear in the SUBJECTS section of the school counselor's STEPnotes™. Examples of these subjects include behavioral problems in the classroom, and in-school suspension. In addition, the word, "client" is replaced with the word, "student" throughout the school counselor STEPnotes™. There are also unique checkboxes in the EVALUATION portion of the school counselor STEPnotes™, which ask if a parent, teacher, or other school administrator was involved in the counseling process.

Career Counseling STEPnotes™: includes a customized assessment scale specifically for career counseling clients as well as particular areas focused on career assessment and career planning materials. Users can upload additional career materials, such as cover letters, resumes, and career assessment results for each client and session. This system provides counseling theories focused on the career counseling process in the THERAPEUTIC TOOLS section.

The school and career counseling options of STEPnotes™ offer the same streamlined features of the original online version, but in addition consider domain-specific issues. STEPnotes™, Inc. is also in the process of creating a note taking system for clinical supervisors. This will allow supervisors to more effectively document supervision sessions. Also in the process are customized STEPnotes™ for couples, families and group counseling sessions.

The STEPnotes™ e-tool was created in February 2013; these additional features are on schedule to be completed in early 2014.

Chapter 9:
PAPER VERSION OF
STEPnotes™

STEPnotes™: Individual Counseling

Name of Client:

Date:

DOB (Date of Birth):

Reference Number for Client:

Insurance Number:

Medicaid Number:

Medicare Number:

Other:

Length of Session (in minutes or hours):

Location of Session (please check or fill-in):

☐ Office
☐ Home
☐ Community
☐ By phone
☐ Other:

Type of Session (please check or fill-in):

☐ Individual Counseling
☐ Couples/Marital Counseling
☐ Family Counseling
☐ Group Counseling
☐ Employee Assistance (EAP) Session
☐ Other:

CPT Code (for insurance billing purposes check one):

☐ 90791 (diagnostic evaluation and assessment)
☐ 90832 (counseling session—actual time of 16 to 37 minutes)
☐ 90834 (counseling session—actual time of 38 to 52 minutes)
☐ 90837 (counseling session—actual time of 53 minutes or more)
☐ 90846 (family counseling without the client present)
☐ 90847 (family counseling with the client present or couples therapy)
☐ 90849 (multiple-family group counseling)
☐ 90853 (group counseling)
☐ 90785 (add-on code for interactive complexity and 30 to 74 minutes)
☐ 90839 (crisis counseling—actual time of 30 to 74 minutes)
☐ 90840 (crisis counseling—additional blocks of time of up to 30 minutes each)

Subjects and Symptoms:

What did the client discuss? What was the focus of the session? What behaviors did the client display during the session? How were the client's affect, mood, and cognitions? What symptoms did the client report?

MENU OF SUBJECT(S) DISCUSSED DURING
SESSION (check all that apply):

- [ ] Abuse
- [ ] Academic problem(s)
- [ ] Addiction
- [ ] Alcohol abuse
- [ ] Alcoholism
- [ ] Anxiety
- [ ] Behavioral problem
- [ ] Career problems
- [ ] Cognitive problems
- [ ] Depression
- [ ] Divorce
- [ ] Domestic violence
- [ ] Drug abuse
- [ ] Eating disorder
- [ ] Emotional abuse
- [ ] Empty nest
- [ ] Family problems
- [ ] Financial issues
- [ ] Gambling addiction
- [ ] Grief/loss
- [ ] Health problems
- [ ] Infertility
- [ ] Infidelity
- [ ] Internet addiction
- [ ] Legal issues

- [ ] Life transition(s)
- [ ] Marital problems
- [ ] Menopause
- [ ] Mental abuse
- [ ] Miscarriage
- [ ] Mood cycles
- [ ] Panic attacks
- [ ] Phobias
- [ ] Physical abuse
- [ ] Porn addiction
- [ ] Rape
- [ ] Relationship issues
- [ ] Relationship violence
- [ ] Retirement
- [ ] School problems
- [ ] Self-esteem issues
- [ ] Self-mutilation
- [ ] Sexual problems
- [ ] Sexual abuse
- [ ] Sexual assault
- [ ] Social anxiety
- [ ] Substance abuse
- [ ] Trauma
- [ ] Work-related issues
- [ ] Other:

MENU OF SYMPTOMS
Emotional Symptoms:

- ☐ Aggressive
- ☐ Alexithymia
- ☐ Angry
- ☐ Anhedonia
- ☐ Animated
- ☐ Annoyed
- ☐ Anxious
- ☐ Apathetic
- ☐ Bashful
- ☐ Bored
- ☐ Cautious
- ☐ Confident
- ☐ Confused
- ☐ Curious
- ☐ Depressed
- ☐ Determined
- ☐ Disappointed
- ☐ Discouraged
- ☐ Disgusted
- ☐ Embarrassed
- ☐ Enthusiastic
- ☐ Envious
- ☐ Ecstatic

- ☐ Excited
- ☐ Exhausted
- ☐ Fearful
- ☐ Frightented
- ☐ Frustrated
- ☐ Guilty
- ☐ Happy
- ☐ Helpless
- ☐ Hopeful
- ☐ Hopeless
- ☐ Hostile
- ☐ Humiliated
- ☐ Hurt
- ☐ Hysterical
- ☐ Irritated
- ☐ Jealous
- ☐ Lonely
- ☐ Loved
- ☐ Loving
- ☐ Negative
- ☐ Optimistic
- ☐ Miserable
- ☐ Pained

- ☐ Paranoid
- ☐ Peaceful
- ☐ Proud
- ☐ Puzzled
- ☐ Regretful
- ☐ Relieved
- ☐ Sad
- ☐ Satisfied
- ☐ Shocked
- ☐ Shy
- ☐ Sorry
- ☐ Stubborn
- ☐ Sure
- ☐ Surprised
- ☐ Suspicious
- ☐ Thoughtful
- ☐ Uncertain
- ☐ Undecided
- ☐ Withdrawn
- ☐ Worthless
- ☐ Other:

☐ More details regarding emotional symptoms:

Behavioral Symptoms:

- [ ] Agitation
- [ ] Avoiding certain things/people
- [ ] Crying
- [ ] Decreased need for sleep
- [ ] Eating less
- [ ] Eating more
- [ ] Elevated mood
- [ ] Encopresis
- [ ] Enuresis
- [ ] Heightened energy
- [ ] Hyperarousal
- [ ] Increased need for sleep
- [ ] Increased physical activity
- [ ] Increased risk taking
- [ ] Increased spending
- [ ] Insomnia
- [ ] Irritability
- [ ] Isolating from others
- [ ] Lethargy
- [ ] Mania
- [ ] Minimal eye contact
- [ ] Neglecting responsibilities
- [ ] Nervous habits
- [ ] Poor impulse control
- [ ] Poor self-care
- [ ] Pressured speech
- [ ] Procrastinating
- [ ] Psychomotor retardation
- [ ] Repeating certain behaviors
- [ ] Restlessness
- [ ] Sleeping less
- [ ] Sleeping more
- [ ] Spending money
- [ ] Trichotillomania
- [ ] Using alcohol
- [ ] Using drugs
- [ ] Other:

- [ ] More details regarding behavioral symptoms:

Cognitive Symptoms:

- ☐ Alexithymia
- ☐ Anxious thoughts
- ☐ Constant worry
- ☐ Flight of ideas/thoughts
- ☐ Inability to concentrate
- ☐ Increased self-esteem
- ☐ Irrational thoughts
- ☐ Lack of concentration
- ☐ Lack of focus
- ☐ Memory problems
- ☐ Negative thoughts
- ☐ Poor judgment
- ☐ Racing thoughts
- ☐ Tangential thoughts
- ☐ Other:

☐ More details regarding cognitive symptoms:

Physical Symptoms:

- ☐ Accelerated heart rate
- ☐ Allergies
- ☐ Body aches and pains
- ☐ Chest pain
- ☐ Constipation
- ☐ Diarrhea
- ☐ Dizziness
- ☐ Fatigue
- ☐ Frequent colds
- ☐ Headaches
- ☐ Hives
- ☐ Injury(ies)
- ☐ Lethargy
- ☐ Loss of sex drive
- ☐ Nausea
- ☐ Skin rashes
- ☐ Sleep disturbance
- ☐ Sweating
- ☐ Trembling
- ☐ Tremors
- ☐ Weight gain
- ☐ Other:

☐ More details regarding physical symptoms:

Therapeutic Tools and Interventions:

What did the counselor do? What therapy approach was used? What therapeutic tools and or interventions did the counselor apply?

MENU OF THERAPY APPROACHES (check all that apply):

☐ Adlerian Therapy
☐ Art Therapy
☐ Behavioral Therapy
☐ Cognitive-Behavioral Therapy (CBT)
☐ Critical Incident Stress Debriefing (CISD)
☐ Dialectical Behavior Therapy (DBT)
☐ Eye Movement Desensitization Reprocessing (EMDR)
☐ Existential Therapy
☐ Family Systems Therapy
☐ Gestalt Therapy
☐ Hypnotherapy
☐ Humanistic Therapy
☐ Narrative Therapy
☐ Neurolinguistic Programming (NLP)
☐ Person-Centered Therapy
☐ Psychoanalytic Therapy
☐ Reality Therapy
☐ Solution-Focused Therapy
☐ Transactional Analysis
☐ Trauma Focused CBT
☐ Other approach:

MENU OF ACTION VERBS:

☐ Acknowledged:	☐ Distinguished:	☐ Normalized:
☐ Addressed:	☐ Encouraged:	☐ Notified:
☐ Aligned:	☐ Evaluated:	☐ Obtained:
☐ Analyzed:	☐ Examined:	☐ Observed:
☐ Asked:	☐ Expanded:	☐ Planned:
☐ Assessed:	☐ Explained:	☐ Prepared:
☐ Brainstormed:	☐ Explored:	☐ Presented:
☐ Compared:	☐ Expressed:	☐ Processed:
☐ Completed:	☐ Generated:	☐ Proposed:
☐ Confronted:	☐ Guided:	☐ Recommended:
☐ Consulted with:	☐ Helped:	☐ Reflected:
☐ Contacted:	☐ Identified:	☐ Reframed:
☐ Constructed:	☐ Illustrated:	☐ Reinforced:
☐ Contrasted:	☐ Implemented:	☐ Reviewed:
☐ Coordinated:	☐ Improved:	☐ Revised:
☐ Created:	☐ Increased:	☐ Role played:
☐ Decreased:	☐ Integrated:	☐ Scheduled:
☐ Defined:	☐ Interpreted:	☐ Summarized:
☐ De-escalated:	☐ Led:	☐ Supported:
☐ Defined:	☐ Linked:	☐ Targeted:
☐ Demonstrated:	☐ Listed:	☐ Taught:
☐ Described:	☐ Maintained:	☐ Trained:
☐ Designed:	☐ Managed:	☐ Used:
☐ Developed:	☐ Mediated:	☐ Utilized:
☐ Differentiated:	☐ Modeled:	☐ Verbalized:
☐ Discussed:	☐ Monitored:	☐ Voiced:
		☐ Other:

Evaluation/Assessment:

What is your evaluation of the client's progress? How engaged is the client in treatment? Is the client compliant, resistant, or stuck? What is your assessment of the client? Are they working towards their goals or stuck, experiencing resistance, etc.?

MENU OF ASSESSMENTS:

- [ ] Client is engaged in therapy
- [ ] Client is resistant to therapy
- [ ] Client is guarded
- [ ] Client is withdrawn
- [ ] Client is open
- [ ] Client is committed
- [ ] Client is minimizing
- [ ] Client is compliant with interventions and treatment plan
- [ ] Client is meeting therapeutic goals
- [ ] Client is "stuck"/has problems moving forward in therapy
- [ ] Client's mental status impedes therapeutic process
- [ ] Other:

Assessment of Functioning: (grade the client from 1-10 using the Client's Current Level of Functioning Scale. Report that number here_____)

Plan:

What is the treatment plan or the goals set out for the next session and future sessions? What homework did you assign between sessions?

MENU OF TREATMENT GOALS:

- ☐ Client will acknowledge:
- ☐ Client will address:
- ☐ Client will attend:
- ☐ Client will build:
- ☐ Client will change:
- ☐ Client will communicate:
- ☐ Client will decrease:
- ☐ Client will develop:
- ☐ Client will draw:
- ☐ Client will exhibit:
- ☐ Client will explore:
- ☐ Client will express:
- ☐ Client will gain:
- ☐ Client will identify:
- ☐ Client will implement:
- ☐ Client will improve:

- ☐ Client will increase:
- ☐ Client will list:
- ☐ Client will maintain:
- ☐ Client will manage:
- ☐ Client will monitor:
- ☐ Client will practice:
- ☐ Client will process:
- ☐ Client will reduce:
- ☐ Client will replace:
- ☐ Client will share:
- ☐ Client will show:
- ☐ Client will structure:
- ☐ Client will utilize:
- ☐ Client will verbalize:
- ☐ Client will write:
- ☐ Other:

Therapist's Signature: _____

Date: ____ / ____ / _____

CLIENT'S CURRENT LEVEL OF FUNCTIONING SCALE

1 to 2: <u>POOR LEVEL OF FUNCTIONING AND STATUS OF CLIENT IS CRITICAL</u>. Client cannot be safe from doing harm to either self or others and has a plan to commit harm; or client is unable to participate in counseling due to bizarre behaviors, poor communication or major problems with functioning. In addition, client may be in need of more critical services due to lack of food and/or shelter, medical condition that needs more immediate attention, or engagement in significant risk-taking behaviors. Client may be actively psychotic, suicidal with a plan or homicidal with a plan. Level of functioning is very low given the client's current mental, physical and emotional states. More than individual/outpatient counseling is needed at this point given the client's mental health needs.

3 to 4: <u>LOW LEVEL OF FUNCTIONING AND ADDITIONAL SERVICES MAY BE NEEDED</u>. Client has some thoughts of hurting self or hurting others but no clear plan; or client has limited ability to engage in counseling due to odd behaviors, poor communication, addictive behaviors or problems outside of mental health issues (such as joblessness) that interfere with functioning. Client is "stuck" in terms of moving forward in therapy and is having problems making any

progress due to lack of insight and/or motivation. Counseling goals cannot be set given the client's low level of functioning. Client may benefit from a referral outside of individual/outpatient therapy that assists with additional mental, emotional and physical health concerns.

5 to 6: MODERATE LEVEL OF FUNCTIONING: GOALS ARE BEING SET. Client is able to engage in counseling; has some problems with overall functioning due to depressive thoughts, anxious thoughts, compulsions or other mental health concerns. Client has some difficulty with completing homework assignments, following through on suggestions or fully participating in the counseling process. Or, client has not been able to set counseling goals given need to more fully process thoughts and feelings. Client is making little progress given limited insights about self and others or due to a need to further share and explore the issues that are causing problems for the client. Client may exhibit either an uncertain or low motivation for change given symptoms client is experiencing. Goals have been set, but client is having difficulty either setting goals or meeting the goals.

7 to 8: GOOD LEVEL OF FUNCTIONING: MANY GOALS ARE BEING MET. Client is showing improvement and overall functioning is improving due to lessening thoughts and feelings associated with depression, anxiety or other mental health issues. Client follows through on most homework

assignments or suggestions and often engages in the counseling process. Client's insights and motivations are increasing. Client appears more comfortable with the counseling process and is gaining insights about self, learning new coping strategies and shows motivation for change and improvement in overall functioning. Client is meeting some counseling goals; is working to implement new tools and strategies discussed in counseling.

9 to 10: <u>HIGH LEVEL OF FUNCTIONING: GOALS ARE BEING MET</u>. Improvement in client's overall functioning is evident and sustainable given client's insights, client's ability to utilize coping skills and client's engagement in the therapy process. Client is engaging in counseling and is meeting counseling goals. Plans for termination of counseling can be discussed.

Additional information: (e.g., if client is suicidal, was there a contract for safety or was the client admitted to the hospital?)

About the Author

Dr. Rhonda Sutton is a licensed professional counselor and counselor supervisor with over 25 years of experience. She runs her own private practice in North Carolina, and also serves as an adjunct professor in the Counselor Education Program at North Carolina State University. As a supervisor for counselors-in-training, she found that many of her supervisees requested guidance in taking progress notes. Given this need, Dr. Sutton developed STEPnotes™ so that counselors and counselors-in-training could have a better method for writing their progress notes.

53244826R00056

Made in the USA
Middletown, DE
11 July 2019